Right Here Right Now Enjoy!

Madeleine Carol Evans Tinsley

All rights reserved including the right to reproduce this book in any form or by any means excepting brief quotes used in reviews without the prior written consent of the author.

Right Here Right Now Enjoy! © *2013*
Madeleine Carol Evans Tinsley

Word in Due Season Publishing, LLC
P.O. BOX 210921
Auburn Hills, Michigan 48321-0921

COVER DESIGN BY ET GRAPHIX

ISBN 13: 978-0-9829686-8-0

Printed in the United States of America

THIS BOOK IS DEDICATED TO MY FIVE CHILDREN AND MY GRANDCHILDREN.

I give a heartfelt thanks for their love, support and prayers. For all my dreams, hopes and wishes to walk in purpose and to make my destiny happen with lots of love and light along the way.

Madeleine Carol Evans Tinsley

Table of Contents

One Source, Many Channels 4
Silence 5
Happiness 6
Morning Sunshine 7
Blue 8
Listen 9
Guardian Angels 10
Early in the Morning 11
A Mystery 12
Chocolate Rivers 13
Out of Brown Comes Green 15
Sunshine in My Hand 16
Treasure Chest 16
I Rest 17
Happy 18
The Rose Bush 19
All for Me 20
Let Me Be 20
I See the Blue 21
Open Your Heart to Love 22
Colors in the Sky 23
Raining Gold 24
Gifts 25
I Feel God 26

5:30 AM	27
Happiness	28
Every Year	29
Dusty Peach Clouds	29
Senses	30
Far Away	30
Mint Coffee and Garlic Eggs	32
Mind Games	33
A Beacon of Light	34
Winter	35
Crystal Atmosphere	36
Cold White Feathers	37
Old Whiskey Bottles	38
Tiny Tracks	39
God Wash Me Clean	40
Guiding Light	40
Prayer	41
Angels	42
Gentle and Steady	43
Forever Grateful	44
Stumps and Garbage Cans	45
It's a Beige World	47
My Spirit	48
I Met Talent by Chance	49
Always	49
Alabama	50
Reality Check	51
Happy	52
Summer Love	52
The Old House	53

Desire	54
The Spirit	55
Quiet Time	56
Neighborhood Park	57
Thank You Jesus	58
Summer	59
A Break	60
Gentle Spirit	61
My Gifts	62
The Spirit of God	63
Beautiful	64
What Now	65
Rainbows and Waterfalls	66
A Piece of Blue	67
Mist of Mystery	68
Thank You	69
A Hill, A House and a Tree	70
My Son and Me	71
Snickers (Laurie's Dog)	72
Yellow	73
Light	74
I Am	74
Perks	75
Grandma	76
Quietness	77
Ice Cream Heaven	78
Flash Light	79

One Source, Many Channels

Life is real
As real as can be
If you don't believe it
Take a look at me.

I'm here. I'm there.
I'm all over the place.
Because of my age, they say you should slow your pace.

Slow my pace?
They must be joking!
In spite of my age,
I am going to keep on stroking.

I am going to live my life to the fullest each day,
And try to spread love and light all along the way.

I will live and love and smell the flowers,
As I dance and play in warm summer showers.

The beaches, the oceans, the beautiful hills
I pray each day to God for my cup to be filled.

I intend to give as much as I get
And spread joy and peace before the final sunset.

Silence

Why is this silence creeping up on me?
It's getting louder and louder - as loud as can be.

There is a sadness that comes with it,
I don't know why.
I can't figure it out
And I won't even try.

Silence to me has always been a good thing.
But with this silence, I don't know what it might bring.

So as I sit here and quietly anticipate,
I will listen to the silence as I patiently wait.

Happiness

Angels and butterflies,

Oh, what a joy!

Like sunshine and wind chimes

And my grandchild's first toy.

The happiness they bring,

I cannot explain.

It's like the feeling I get

In a warm summer rain.

Morning Sunshine

What a morning!
What a day!
Everything is going my way!

Bright yellow sheets on my bed,
Soft rays of sunshine
Kiss my forehead.

I'm in my bedroom,
One of my favorite spots.
I'm reading a book about what we should do
And what we should not.

As I listen to the alarm clock tick,
To this book I cannot stick.

I would rather be here and contemplate,
The wonder of this day in a quiet state.

Blue

Blue through the gray
With touches of green,
It's one side of winter
Not often seen.

The sun is shining
So light and bright
Making long dark shadows
Left and right.

Winter wonderland they say.
Just like the beauty I see today.

I love the winters in my home town.
It helps me to remember that God is always around.

From season to season the colors vary.
Sometimes soft and subtle, sometimes profound
Like a bright red cherry.

No matter what the colors, they are always true.
There is no way I could ever be blue.

Listen

God has a way of
Making things right.
That's why He keeps us
All in His sight.

The only thing we have to do,
Is listen to his plan and follow it through.

How do I listen?
I ask myself.
For that is the mystery
To all our wealth.

We listen with our mind.
We listen with our heart.
Because God and these two
Are not far apart.

Listen!

Guardian Angels

Guardian angels all around me
As far as my spirit can see.

Guardian angels all around me
To help me be what God wants me to be.

Sometimes I look around and I see a face
And I know angels are truly guarding this place.

The sweet smell of roses is in the air
Along with the feeling of God's love and care.

In my heart I know it's true,
What God does for me He will do for you.

Things are not as bad as they seem
Keep on wishing and remember your dreams.

Life is precious in every way
Thank God for giving you another day.

Praise God! Hallelujah!

Early in the Morning

It's early in the morning

There is clean fresh air

It's the time of the morning

That I say my daily prayers .

The birds are singing very loud

The sky is filled with big white clouds.

As I try to keep very still,

My heart is very overjoyed and filled.

Filled with the wonder of my life

Wonders that stay with me from morning to night.

Praise God!

A Mystery

I am not my hair.

I am not my pretty brown eyes.

I am not the excess fat that has taken residence on my thighs.

Regardless of how long you look at the outside of me,

You will never ever know me

Because....

I am a mystery.

Chocolate Rivers

Chocolate rivers and green trees,
Water coming out of rocks, on beautiful mountain sides

Beautiful houses high on hills
Highways running through corn fields

Yellow flowers on the side of the road
Trucks moving slow with their heavy loads

Highways seeming to touch the sky
Mountains and valleys and God and I

I can't even explain how beautiful it is,
This precious treasure this gift of His.

A group of people on a bus,
Riding the highways from dawn to dusk.

Oh what wonderful sights we see!
From all the beauty of God that be!

Beautiful walls of picturesque rocks
Smooth and jagged from bottom to top
High and low, narrow and wide,
As far as you can see and on both sides.

The colors are amazing in every way,
From white and black to coppers and gray.

The design is from the Greatest Artist of all.
It's like the handprint of God on the wall.

One lone patch of yellow flowers on the side of the road
I see
And down the way a field of lavender beneath a variety of trees.

As I sat by the window, on my side of the bus, I inhaled the beauty and let my spirit run free.
As life allowed me to be thankful and grateful for some of God's gifts,
Like a river, a mountain and a tree.

Out of Brown Comes Green

There is an old rose bush that grows behind my yard.
It's been there forever, and the ground is real hard.

Nobody seems to know the rose bush is even there.
If it were not for the sun and the rain, it would get no care.

The rain comes and the sun shines
And the bush keeps growing throughout time.

At the end of winter and the beginning of spring
When I begin to marvel at things,
I look at the bush, and I shake my head.
It looks like it's dying but it's living instead.

Out of the brown comes the green.
It's one of the darnest things I have ever seen.
And out of the green comes the pink,
As pink as pink can be.
And all of this from beginning to end,
Is a beautiful miracle to see.

Sunshine in My Hand

I can hold sunshine in my hand

Carry air in my mouth

Air that keeps me living

Even when I let it out

The sunshine keeps me warm and makes me happy too

Now all I really need is skies of real light blue

Treasure Chest

Golden light reflections from within the darkness glows

It truly is amazing because the darkness seems so cold

But the sunlight has directed a special ray of light

Down through this little opening

That made the darkness bright

One of many simple wonders I notice all the time

In this great big beautiful world

In this treasure chest of mine

I Rest

There is a cloud in the sky and it slowly rolls by

As I sit in my chair and I rest.

My mind is ok but my body says "Nay,

You work me too hard on your quest!"

Your quest to make sure on this present life tour

Everything is done the right way.

From the first crack of dawn, to my very last yawn

Right down to the close of each day.

But I will not complain, at least there's no rain

As I sit in my chair and I rest!

Happy

I am happy but I don't know it.

I am happy but I don't show it.

Something deep within my heart,

Is keeping me and happy apart

I am crying more and I don't know why,

It's like my heart is saying goodbye.

Goodbye to what I thought was an everlasting love.

But maybe the love wasn't sent from above.

The love that I felt was coming from me,

What was coming from the other person, I did not see.

My spirit tells me, "That's ok."

My happiness is being released this day.

There is lots of joy coming my way....joy that will forever stay

In my heart today and every day.

Praise God!

The Rose Bush

As the raindrops fall on the tiny green leaves,

They delicately dance in the warm summer breeze.

It's as if they hear music way down in their roots,

The bright green leaves, the age old stems, and even the brand new roots.

The whole bush seems to jump for joy

As they tremble and bounce all around.

I will never forget that special dance

As the heavy summer rain falls down.

All for Me

Have you ever really looked at the sky,

As a ball of cotton like mist rolls by?

What a beautiful sight to see.

And just think,

It's a gift and it's all for me

Let Me Be

Give me my coffee or

Give me my tea

Give me my quiet

And let me be!

I See the Blue

I see the blue

I see the white

I feel wrapped up in its light.

And with the sky as the guide

And with the Lord by my side

I can go from day to day.

Knowing that He will guide my way,

Through every joy and every tear

In my heart I know God is here.

I am Grateful.

Open Your Heart to Love

Love helps me see,

See all the blessed things that God does for me.

I am at awe

Of the things that I saw

When I opened my heart to the love that is God.

I see rainbows and roses and beautiful trees

It makes me want to get on my knees

And thank the Heavenly Father above for all of His heartfelt precious love.

To God Be the Glory!

Colors in the Sky

Clouds of peach in the sky I see.

Oh, what a beautiful color to me!

As it lights up the space all around,

I sit very still and make not one sound.

I watch the people come and go,

Not one aware of the bright peach glow.

We take for granted the beauty around us,

Beauty so rich it would really astound us.

If only we would really just lift our heads and open our eyes,

There's awesome beauty for us to see not only for you but also for me.

Raining Gold

It's raining gold!

Oh No! That's leaves!

They're falling from my backyard trees.

I looked outside and what did I see?

There was gold falling from the sky for me.

It made me smile.

It made me grin

Until I looked outside again.

At this time I remembered,

We are just one month away from December.

Of course the leaves are falling down.

And soon there will be gold all over town,

Just for the raking.

Gifts

Bees and butterflies,
Flowers and trees,
Oceans and clouds,
And a warm summer breeze
These are just some of the things that I love.
Some of the gifts that are sent from above.

A walk in a park
On a warm spring day,
With a child by my side
That I'm showing the way.
The look on the face of the child is a thrill.
It's so happy and healthy
And so genuinely real.

I love the little hands
As they cling to mine.
These are the gifts
I'll treasure through time.

I Feel God

When I put my hand on a window pane and feel the sunshine, I feel God.

When I hold my hand in the wind, I feel God.

When I feel a new born baby's heartbeat, I feel God.

When I feel love, joy and happiness in my heart, I feel God.

When the water from the ocean rolls on the beach and kisses my feet, I feel God.

I!

Feel!

God!

5:30 AM

It's early in the morning.
I am still in bed.
The birds are loudly singing.
The song swirls around my head.

It's been about an hour now, since they started their choir.
And as the time goes by,
The sound goes higher and higher.

It is such a precious sound,
The sound of birds singing.
It puts a sound in my heart,
That throughout the day keeps ringing.

What a way to start my day in this wonderful world of mine!
I pray the birds keep singing all throughout time.

To God be the glory!
Love and Light!

Happiness

Angels are everywhere.
They are just hanging in the air.

When I look at the clouds above,
I think of all the angel's love.

In the quiet stillness of the day,
I can hear the angels play.

When the sun is shining bright,
I see twinkles of angel light.

When the rain is coming down,
There is this precious angel sound.

I love the way they make me feel.
With all their love the world will heal.
One day!

Every Year

Every year will be the year for me,

Much less stress

And much more rest.

God is giving me a better life.

A life complete without the strife.

As I let God have his way,

All my good shall start today!

Praise God!

Dusty Peach Clouds

Dusty peach Clouds in a milky blue sky

Late summer evenings with crickets and fireflies

The smell of cut grass

And the sound of soft jazz

Leaves a feeling that gives me a thrill

As I sit on my porch and be still.

Senses

Butterflies, bees, green grass and yellow flowers,

Oh, what a beautiful morning!

Warm sunshine on my toes

Fresh air in my nose

Soft blue skies that's almost white

A gentle breeze that's just so right

Far Away

Peanut butter and graham crackers too

Grab your coat and put on your shoe.

Out the door and into the car,

We may go near and we may go far.

Oh my goodness, look at the sky!

Maybe we'll drive and maybe we'll fly

Up, up, up and away!

    Maybe, just maybe, we'll come back one day.

My Bath

There is light in the water as it swirls around.

It's making a circle and pulling it down.

Around and around and around it goes

I pull the plug and down it flows

Into the drain as fast as it can

Somewhere down in unknown land.

Now to clean the tub is my next task

Since I've just finished taking my bath.

Mint Coffee and Garlic Eggs

Mint coffee and garlic eggs,
What a delightful treat!
It was early one Saturday morning,
And I wanted something different to eat.

I was not in some great castle
Or some mansion on a hill,
But knowing that I was a gourmet at heart,
Gave me such a thrill!

My imagination began to soar
And the anticipation was high,
Because I knew at this point
My only limit was the sky.

I made note of all the ingredients I had
And mentally put them together.
Now I have a meal I can enjoy today
And also forever.

Mind Games

Water flows over hot coals and freezes instantly.

Lilies on a lily pad get up and walk away.

Butterflies take on big wings and attack a chicken hawk.

Today's teens are praised and cheered for the good and kind things they do.

Is "mind" dictating what I say, or is this coming from you?

A Beacon of Light

I love the Lord with all that I have
Even though the world around me is very sad.

I will get over the stress and worry too,
Because God is showing me what to do.

He fills my days with lots of joy.
I am as happy as a child with a toy.

The skies are blue and each day is new.
How I will move on, I have no clue.

I intend to make the most of my life.
I will start by leaving behind the worry and strife.

And I will live and love,
And become a beacon of light.
With the help of God, it will be alright.

Winter

There were tiny, tiny diamonds

From a very rich Father that lives way up high.

They fell upon a pure white ground

And beautiful sparkles could be seen all around.

The air was cold and the sun was out

And there were quiet sounds all about.

It was early January 2004

And my love for winter

Grew more and more.

Crystal Atmosphere

In this crystal atmosphere, the beautiful ice is here
The trees are all clear.

The word beautiful does not completely explain
When all the trees are covered with freezing rain.

Such a wondrous sight to see
Like a child we think, how can this be?

I have heard about winter wonderland
Now I truly understand.
There is no creation in our mind
That could outdo this gift of Thine.

What an awesome display of Thy handiwork this day!

To God be the Glory!

Cold White Feathers

Cold white feathers from the sky
Look at them float, look at them fly
Falling like a whirlwind from on high.
Down and down and down they fall
Where a pure white blanket covers all.
The house tops, the cars and especially the ground
There are cold white feathers all around.
Of course, I know it is really snow.
I am just sitting here enjoying this beautiful show.

Old Whiskey Bottles

I am going for my morning stroll.

It's good for my health, or so I'm told.

I decide to walk through the neighborhood.

My time is limited, so close is good.

I pass old whiskey bottles and broken concrete,

Torn screen doors and lawns that are not so neat.

Street signs knocked down,

And young men acting a clown

This is what I see as I walk through the hood.

I am not complaining, let that be understood.

I'm just trying to think of what I can do,

So things will be better

Next time I pass through,

The hood!

Tiny Tracks

As I stand by the window and look out,

It is definitely winter

There is no doubt.

Very quiet and very cold,

Just listen to the wind that blows.

There are tiny tracks through the snow

Left by the neighbor's cat, at least I think so.

The trees are covered and so are the cars

And snow is falling down like little white stars.

My back yard is covered under a pure white sheet.

The beauty that I see just can't be beat.

I stand quietly here as I pray,

I thank God for another Christmas Day.

God Wash Me Clean

As I open my consciousness
To the mighty cleansing tide of Your Spirit,
Wash me clean.

Guiding Light

How gently you watch over me
In everything I do.
It never fails
Whatever the situation,
You always get me through.
Sometimes it seems I'm so uptight.
There is no answer,
Not in my sight.
And then as I quiet my spirit down,
I feel Your Presence all around.
You are all around me day and night.
Your Spirit is my guiding light.

Prayer

Jesus! Please help me this day.

Help me please to find my way.

I know I can if I just trust,

And keep my faith as I know I must,

My heart has hope of many great things.

I pray my faith will always have wings.

Angels

Angels are everywhere.

They are just hanging in the air.

When I look at the clouds above,

I think of all of the angel's love.

In the quiet stillness of the day,

I can hear the angels play.

When the sun is shining bright,

I see twinkles of angel light.

When the rain is coming down,

There is this precious angel sound.

I love the way they made me feel,

With all of their love, the world will heal.

One day!

Gentle and Steady

Gentle and steady the rain comes down,
Raining blessings all over town.
God will bring peace in our hearts again.
God will do it like nothing else can.

It will be like a soft summer rain
Or the light golden glow of a fireside flame.
The only thing you have to do
Is to your own heart be true.

No one else can show you the way
To bring joy and happiness in your life today.

Be Blessed!

Forever Grateful

I am forever grateful and forever thankful
For all that You do for me.
I am grateful for this day and thankful that I know Thee.
I am grateful that I can feel and thankful that I can see.

I am grateful for the mercy
That You extend to me each day.
I am thankful for all the blessings
 I receive along the way.

I am grateful for all the love
That has come into my life.
I am thankful for the lessons
That I learned from all the strife.

I am grateful for the birds and bees
And all the flowers too.
I am thankful for the knowledge
That I know all of this is You.

I am grateful for the stars at night
That shine and light my way.
I am thankful for the morning
That shows forth another day.

Now as I make this journey through this life of mine,
I will be forever grateful
This day and all throughout time

Stumps and Garbage Cans

Stumps and garbage cans, old cars and collard greens,

Windows boarded and doors with no screens

"Is Brenda getting up?" A young lady hollers

(to an older lady in an upstairs window)

As she walks down the middle of the street

On her way to the school bus stop.

Everything is so green and freshly washed,

After a night of heavy rain.

But as I look closer and take it all in,

The leaves have started to turn colors again.

The squirrels are busy scampering

Over sidewalks and fences.

The birds seem so excited

As they visit from house to house

As I wonder where the summer went.

The quietness of the morning speaks loudly to my ear.

I wish I could record the sounds that I hear.

Birds chirping, babies crying,

The smell of bacon is so strong,

I can almost hear it frying.

I hear laughter, I feel love,

It comes from around me,

It comes from above.

Thanks to the powers that be,

The One that gave this day to me.

It's a Beige World

It's a beige world, I am just beginning to see.

There is dark beige and light beige all around me.

Beige clothes and beige cars as far as the eye can see.

I never knew there was so much beige.

I never gave it a thought.

Beige is a soft color a quiet color,

A color with lots of power.

I think when I plant my garden this year…

I will plant me some pretty beige flowers.

My Spirit

Early morning readings

Of a book from yesteryear,

Help me realize

That life is precious and so dear.

The things that I have read

In this quiet morning time,

Have opened up my mind

To more wonder and more rhyme.

The things that I don't know

Outweigh the things I do.

So I sit and ponder knowledge

In the early morning dew.

My heart is filled with joy

And hope of things to come,

As my spirit anticipates the beat of distant drums.

I Met Talent by Chance

I was on vacation a short time ago
I met some young people they were all go, go, go.
They were ready to help and they were willing to do
Whatever it takes to make success come through.

These were bright young people
On a solid foundation.
Getting a real strong grip
On the world of information.

There was something real special about this group.
It had something to do with respect and truth.
One day I am sure I will hear great things,
As their desires and wishes begin to take wings.

Always

There is always a light glowing,

God showing me the way.

As He keeps and guides me

All through the day!

Alabama

Butterflies as big as birds,
As pretty as they can be.
Alabama in the afternoon,
What a beautiful site to see!

The sun is bright, and my spirit is light,
As I try to take it all in.
There are tall pecan trees all over the place,
Their leaves blowing gently in the wind.

I watch lizards scampering over plants and walls.
I keep my camera so I can capture it all.

The people are friendly, they always wave.
That's one memory I will try to save.

I have tasted the peaches I have tasted the pears
That I personally picked from the tree.
I have taken a long ride down to the country
And it makes my spirit feel free.

Reality Check

Once upon a time, a rose bush was there.
But all throughout time the rose bush got no care
People came and went without the slightest hint
That the rose bush is a part of God
And it needs more than just the sod.
It needs the rain and sunshine too
It even needs the evening dew

This reminds me of you and I
And how we care for ourselves as time goes by.
We are also a part of God
Even if some might think that's odd.
We need care every day
And we need care in every way.

Care in what we choose to eat.
Care in where we choose to sleep.
Care in the thoughts that we think.
Care in our choices when we are near the brink.

Do we choose love or do we choose hate?
Should this be just a friend or should this be my mate?
Choice is the question, there is no doubt.
How we make that choice, that's what this is all about.

I've made up my mind the very next time
I have a choice to make,
I am going to be still
I am going to be patient
And I am going to pray for heaven sakes.

Happy

Happy during the day light hours

Happy during the darkness that follows

Happy to be free to be…

And know my happiness

Depends on me.

Summer Love

Butterflies and bumble bees

Pretty flowers and bright green trees

That's what summer is all about

And I do love it

Without a doubt

The Old House

My tenants just moved and left me alone.

Now I have to survive all on my own.

I am an old house by the side of the road

Surrounded by birds and crickets and toads.

Nobody knows how lonely I am.

Everyone just walks by

Every Tom, Dick and Sam.

I miss all the noise from the girls and boys,

Especially when they fuss and fight over toys.

But I know on the inside I will be just fine

As I stand and look out at the passing of time.

Desire

Oh, to be what I desire to be!

Oh, to know what I desire to be!

Oh, to thank You for filling that desire for me!

Oh, to have what I desire to have!

Oh, to know what I desire to have!

And then to have and have until

I can give and give

To others that might

Desire to have.

The Spirit

The pink fades back into the green,

And the green fades into the brown.

The rest is left up to the Spirit

The Spirit that lives in the ground.

The Spirit that works its magic each day

In ways that no one can see.

The Spirit that makes sure we have beautiful things;

Summer, fall, winter and spring.

Things like butterflies, flowers and bees

If you are wondering about what Spirit I speak,

It's the Spirit that no one sees.

Quiet Time

The quietness of this day -

Oh, how I wish it would stay.

Stay until the joy of noise –

Like Christmas time with girls and boys.

Or stay until another season –

That makes more sense,

More rhyme, more reason.

As I listen to the sound –

The quietness is so profound.

It makes me think,

It makes me ponder,

About everything from

Shadows to thunder.

Another day in this life of mine –

Another moment of quiet time.

Neighborhood Park

Sunshine and butterflies

Green grass and blue skies

A bridge over waters

Very tall trees

Beginning to bud into

So many leaves

Wide open spaces

Smiling faces

Children's laughter fills the air

When so many others don't even know it's there,

I care!

Thank You Jesus

Thank you Jesus for love and light.
Thank you Jesus for day and night.
Thank you for the privilege of loving you.
Thank you for being with me in all that I do.

I am so blessed from day to day.
Sometimes I don't know what to say.
Then my mind says you have a duty
To acknowledge and share all of God's beauty.
The beauty of His presence in everyday things;
From the sound of music to the flowers in spring.
A little child's laughter and the smile on that child's face
The joy and beauty of children of every race.

God is with us believe it or not.
And to be quite honest, He's all we've got,
To help us and guide us along our way.

Don't put your faith up on a shelf.
God wants you to be good to yourself.
Trust and believe in all that you do
And know in your heart that God will get you through.
Thank you God for Jesus!

Summer

One eye open and not quite in focus

From my open window the smell of lotus

My senses tell me the hour has come

To rise again and watch the world go to and from

As beams of warm yellow through my window do show

I hear a voice say, "I'm not calling you again hit the flo!"

With one last yawn and one extra-long stretch,

I force myself to hit the deck.

A Break

There is a break in the clouds. There is a break I say.

I know that's not strange, it happens every day.

I just looked up and noticed it there

As the clouds slowly moved to God knows where.

Part of it's pink and part of it's blue

There is a little gray mixed in there too.

Little things like this, they catch my eye.

But please don't ask me to tell you why…

Give me a break!!!

Gentle Spirit

How gently You watch over me in everything I do.
It never fails whatever the situation,
You always get me through.
Sometimes it seems I'm so uptight.
There is no answer, not in my sight.
And then as I quiet my spirit down,
I feel your presence all around.
You are all around me day and night.
Your Spirit is my guiding light.
Praise God!

My Gifts

There are pink and purple, doll babies and flowers,

And beautiful music for hours and hours.

There are bright yellow leaves all over the ground

And red leaves and gold leaves still falling down.

There is a chill in the air

And something else too…

A soft clear voice, saying "These are gifts I give you."

The Spirit of God

God's Spirit is moving.
Tell me it's not.
I will tell you
You're lying.

Tell me you can't see it.
I will tell you
You're blind.
I am very sure of what I say.
I see it clearly every day.

The Spirit of God is all around me.
The Spirit of God is in everything I see,
The children, the parents and the powers to be.
So don't be afraid to do the right thing.
Keep trusting the Spirit
And remember to sing.

To God be the Glory!

Beautiful

Touches of beautiful in my life they come –

I am at awe

And amazed at some of the places they come from.

The beauty is medicine for my eyes

Like the pretty white clouds and rainbows in the skies.

It could be a beautiful mountain with a waterfall

Or a forest of green with no ugly at all.

There are many things that make my heart happy

And I pray that will always be.

I also pray that the beauty of this world,

God will always allow me to see.

What Now

Life is such a joy to me, as I live from day to day.
I want so much, I need so much
And I know I can find a way.

I sit and I wonder sometimes by myself
Of things I have not seen or done.
But I must get going, because the day is not just dawning
Although there is still lots of sun.

Sometime in the future the sun will go down,
So I must make the most of this day.
I will dream all my dreams, sing all my songs,
And do all the good I can do.
And regardless of what kind of job that I do,
I want to be proud of my final review.

Rainbows and Waterfalls

It's dead in the middle of winter,
As I sit here and reminisce.
About the warm summer that's coming,
As I enjoy the snowy mist.

It's blowing from the house tops.
It's swirling in the air.
It looks like powdered sugar,
Falling from nowhere.

It makes my heart happy,
As I enjoy this time of year.
I know it won't be long,
Before another season is here.

Every season I try to take in
All that it has to offer.
The sights, the sounds
They are all around;
The green grass and the sky blue waters.

I see rainbows and waterfalls.
I hear music and laughter.
I'm speaking of now,
Not the hereafter.
Life.

A Piece of Blue

A piece of blue behind the green

It's the brightest blue I ever seen.

The rest of the sky is a misty gray.

It has been that way most of the day.

Every so often there are puffs of white.

Before you know it they are out of sight.

There is the blue again.

The clouds are very thin.

As they slowly move across the sky,

I take it all in with my inner eye.

The beauty I see I can't explain.

It all came about after a gentle spring rain.

Mist of Mystery

What is this mist of mystery?

What is it I feel, what is it I see?

Quietness that is very loud,

I am sitting still, my head is bowed.

It's as if there is something I am anticipating.

I know not what it is but I am still waiting.

I know this is just a state of mind,

But there are answers I would like to find.

So this mist will go away

And the mystery will be solved for all one day.

Thank You

I thank you Jesus for birds, for love and light,

Thank You for favor and blessings, for lessons learned

And corners turned,

Thank You for things I see and things I want to see

And for You making it all possible for me.

I love you Lord with all my heart, with all my might,

With all that I am and all that I pray to be.

I praise you!

Thank you for this year,

The year that we are in.

Thank you for friends and for being thin.

Thank you for joy and feeling, oh boy!

Thank you for hope and helping me cope

And for making my way a brighter day.

I am because God is!

Thank you!

A Hill, A House and a Tree

A hill, a house and a tree

Everyday that's all I see.

A hill, a house and a tree

I listen for sounds,

As I sit here and frown

And ask the Lord why must this be?

Why must I sit here without a smile;

Feeling and acting like a lost spoiled child?

I need sunshine and pretty green meadows,

Pretty flowers and babbling brooks,

A quiet place to meditate and maybe even write a book.

Hopefully, it will be a bestselling book

About a hill, a house and a tree.

My Son and Me

Lord, have mercy on my son

And Lord, have mercy on another one.

Lord that other one is me.

I act like I just cannot see.

With all the knowledge and wisdom from You,

I act like I don't know what to do.

I sit around with my head hung down

And on my face there's even a frown.

In my heart I know that's not the way

You would have me spend my day.

I hear You say lift up your head,

And spend your day with Me instead.

I lift mine eyes unto the hills from whence cometh my help.

Psalm 121:1

Snickers (Laurie's Dog)

I can almost hear her barking,

As she lay in a silent state.

I stop for just a moment,

As I be still and wait.

It's almost as if she knows of the sadness that I feel,

As I go to the back door

And look up on the hill.

She was a constant companion,

So loving and so free.

All I can do now is say,

Lord I let Your will be!

Yellow

I am wrapped up in yellow all by myself.

I am wrapped up in yellow up on lonely shelf.

Yellow is bright, like my spirit.

Yellow is why I'm wrapped all up in it.

I am trying real hard not to be sad

And yellow is a color that makes me feel glad.

Glad that even though I'm all by myself,

I know that God is with me

Here on lonely shelf.

Light

God is beauty.

God is love.

God is light from up above.

Light that shines and shows us His way,

When we open our hearts and sincerely pray.

A light that others might see

The beautiful bright glow of God shining through me!

Love and Light.

I Am

I am

The sum total of all

And

None of it!

I am that

I am

As God

Sees fit!

Perks

A rose is God's autograph

That's what someone told me.

A rose is such a beautiful thing,

At least that's what I see.

I am walking through a wooded area

With a long winding path.

Along the way I see a red bird

Taking his daily bath.

I see many flowers of many colors

And many other things.

As I continue my walk, the bird begins to sing.

The melody is soft and sweet,

As I continue along the way.

The sound of the quietness goes straight to my heart

As I begin to thank God for this day.

What a gift, what a joy

To be in the woods as they talk!

I accept it as just one of the perks,

As I go on my morning walk.

Grandma

Little people surround my heart

They keep it happy and light.

One thing I hope I can do for them

Is teach them what's wrong and what's right.

I can go from a blank stare

To a wide grin in a minute,

If you show me a picture

With my grandchild in it.

Wide-eyed and curious,

Soft spoken and loud,

Bugs and beetles automatically get a great big "Wow"!

My name has been changed.

My furniture rearranged.

But my heart is still happy

And my spirit still light

Because all of my grands

Are both healthy and bright!

Quietness

In the quietness of the day,

I let my cares float away.

Float away to higher heights

Where little children fly their kites,

Up to a place that is beautiful and still,

Up to a place that is truly real.

I have learned that

That place is within me.

I never knew it was there

Until one day I began to care.

At first it was all about myself,

And as time went by

It was about someone else.

That made my spirit feel happy and light

And within myself I knew that caring was right.

So from this day forward, I promise myself,

I will take my caring off the shelf

And I will share it with love with someone else.

Ice Cream Heaven

Lemon and lime parfait.

The goodness of God is all through my day

And is as special to me as a lemon parfait.

As a child I remember having a dream

Of going to heaven and having ice cream.

Lemon and lime were the two I liked most;

They were always served by the Heavenly Host.

Just a dream of a little girl

That made me feel better

In this old world.

Flash Light

I am your flashlight in the dark

To shine and light your way.

There is no need to be afraid

I will turn your night to day.

Everyone needs a light,

As they travel down their path.

We need a light to find

And complete the simplest task.

I am that flashlight.

Reach for Me.

Turn Me on as well.

 I will shine your light on Heaven

So you won't end up in Hell.

CPSIA information can be obtained
at www.ICGtesting.com
Printed in the USA
LVHW101135290822
727085LV00011B/125